MW01505574

Introduction to

How to
Become a
Water
Walker

Andrew Wommack

© Copyright 2024 – Andrew Wommack

Printed in the United States of America. All rights reserved. No portion of this book may be reproduced, stored in a retrieval system, or transmitted in any form or by any means—electronic, mechanical, photocopy, recording, scanning, or other—except for brief quotations in critical reviews or articles, without the prior written permission of the publisher.

Unless otherwise indicated, all Scripture quotations are taken from the King James Version® of the Bible. Copyright © by the British Crown. Public domain.

All emphasis within Scripture quotations is the author's own.

Published in partnership between Andrew Wommack Ministries and Harrison House Publishers.

Woodland Park, CO 80863 – Shippensburg, PA 17257

ISBN 13 TP: 978-1-59548-669-1

For Worldwide Distribution, Printed in the USA

1 2 3 4 5 6 / 27 26 25 24

Contents

Would you like to get more out of this teaching?

Scan the QR code to access this teaching in video or audio formats to help you dive even deeper as you study.

Accessing the teaching this way will help you get even more out of this booklet.

awmi.net/browse

Introduction

Did you know that God will lead you to do things far beyond your own natural ability? It's true. But there are reasons that some people see the supernatural and others don't. It's not fate or luck. It's not like lightning where you never know when it will strike. God doesn't pick and choose; there are principles we have to follow to see His power manifest. If you don't understand that, you won't experience miracles. But you were made for the supernatural. You were made for the miraculous!

As long as you can live without the miraculous power of God in your life, you will. If your life isn't supernatural, then it's superficial, and one of the traits of being a Christian is the supernatural power of God.

Of course, I'm not saying that God wants you to go *physically* walk on the water. But just like Peter walked on top of the water, you can "walk on top" of your problems and overcome them.

Does anything in your life look overwhelming to you? Is it sickness? How about financial problems or marital problems?

Whatever it is, God wants to release His miracle-working power in you and put you on top. But it's up to you.

The same principles that operated in Peter's life for him to walk on water will work for you too! I've personally seen these truths help countless people. By applying the lessons from this booklet in faith, you will dramatically improve the way you receive from God. You'll learn to step out of the boat—whatever you find security in outside of God—and walk on water!

Chapter 1

The Lord Spoke

One of the first things to understand before you can become a water walker and see the miraculous power of God is that when God says something, He doesn't speak idly. Everything God says, He means!

Consider that as you read this passage:

And straightway Jesus constrained his disciples to get into a ship, and to go before him unto the other side, while he sent the multitudes away. And when he had sent the multitudes away, he went up into a mountain apart to pray: and when the evening was come, he was there alone. But the ship was now in the midst of the sea, tossed with waves: for the wind was contrary.

Matthew 14:22–24

Notice how the Word says that Jesus constrained His disciples to get into the ship and go to the other side. In other words, He didn't say, "Go only halfway and drown."

You see, these disciples didn't think about *who* was telling them to go across the sea. It was by Jesus that this body of water came into existence (Col. 1:16). As a matter of fact, He is the creative Word that God spoke:

In the beginning was the Word, and the Word was with God, and the Word was God. All things were made by him; and without him was not any thing made that was made.

John 1:1, 3

This passage goes on to say that Jesus was that Word (John 1:14). So, God upholds *"all things by the word of his power"* (Heb. 1:3a). This entire world is held together by the integrity of His Word *"and by him all things consist"* (Col. 1:17b). Jesus—the Word—told His disciples, "Get in and go to the other side!" Apparently, they didn't understand who they were dealing with.

Overwhelmed by Circumstances

In Matthew 14, Jesus fed five thousand men with only five loaves and two fish. Taking into account the women and children present, there could have been upwards of ten, fifteen, or even twenty thousand people present! Not only that, but there was more food left over when everyone finished eating than what they started with! However, the disciples didn't keep this miracle in mind when they encountered a storm on the sea. When Jesus came to them, walking on the water, they didn't believe it was Him.

But when they saw him walking upon the sea, they supposed it had been a spirit, and cried out: For they all saw him, and were troubled . . . and they were sore amazed in themselves beyond measure, and wondered. For they considered not the miracle *of the loaves: for their heart was hardened.*

Mark 6:49–52

The disciples were shocked to see Jesus walk on the water because their hearts were hardened! They hadn't considered—meditated, pondered, thought on—the miracle they had just seen. In other words, if the disciples had been focused on what Jesus had done earlier, they wouldn't have been shocked to see Him perform another miracle. They would have been expecting it! Or they could have taken Jesus' words, believed them, and then stilled the storm or walked on the water themselves.

The disciples had already seen Jesus command the wind and waves (Mark 4:39). They could have drawn on that same example and used their faith to calm the present storm as they had seen Jesus do. Maybe you sympathize with the disciples and would say, "But, Andrew, this was a severe storm!" But the disciples wouldn't even have been in this situation if they hadn't been prepared for it. They had been personally trained by the Lord Jesus Christ, and His instructions to go to the other side were not just powerless words. They were more than enough to overcome the storm they were facing on the sea.

"Why Are You Fearful?"

When the Lord spoke to the disciples on the sea, He didn't say, "Guys, I'm sorry. It's My fault. I shouldn't have left you out here by yourself. It's hard to maintain your faith when you're in the midst of a storm." No, Jesus expected them to do better than they did. Although the Lord has compassion on us, it isn't normal to accept our negative circumstances, much less be overwhelmed by them. It may be normal for those who don't believe God, but this isn't the normal Christian life. I believe the Lord expects us to respond better than our unsaved neighbors. We have His promises; we simply need to believe them.

God didn't call you to lose the battle you're facing. He made you to be a world overcomer (1 John 5:4)! Instead of being overcome by your problems, you can overcome your problems by His promises. If the disciples would've had this attitude, they would have had a totally different response and experience on the sea.

In Over Your Head or Playing It Too Safe?

At times, God will tell us to do things that go against the normal flow of nature. He lives in the supernatural realm, and if we are truly following Him, we will too. The Lord wants us to move into the unlimited, supernatural power of God. But we must take Him at His Word to do so.

The Lord will lay things on your heart and give you instructions to accomplish them. It might seem impossible to accomplish because you'll see the wind, the waves, and the storms of life coming against you. Instead of overcoming them, it might appear like you're going to die in the attempt. If you haven't ever been in something like this, where you've gotten in over your head, it's probably because you're playing it too safe. Remember what God has told you—His words have all the power you need to overcome—and get ready to take a step of faith!

Chapter 2

He Would Have Passed Them By

Jesus was praying on a mountain overlooking the Sea of Galilee when His disciples were attempting to cross it. He was in the same storm. He knew what was going on with them because He was going through it too. I believe the reason Jesus came down and started walking on the water was so He could rescue them. But even though He drew near to them, scripture says He *"would have passed by them"* (Mark 6:48).

Think about this: Jesus didn't run out there, waving His arms and yelling, "Guys, don't panic! It's Me! Here I am to save the day!" The Lord revealed Himself to them, but it was their responsibility to call out to Him by faith and make a demand to appropriate His miracle-working power.

The disciples' responsibility to respond in faith to Jesus' presence is a perfect parallel to how God provides miracles for us today. It doesn't matter what our situations are; God knows what we're going through, and He's touched with those same feelings (Heb. 4:15). Jesus is present with us in our circumstances, but we have to reach out in faith to appropriate His power.

Crying out in desperation and pity, saying, "God, don't You love me? Where are You? Do You exist? Do You care?" isn't making a demand on God. If anything, that's tying His hands because it's doubting His Word. In other words, if the disciples were thinking they were going to die, then they were doubting God's Word. This reveals that they weren't aware of how powerful the promise was that Jesus gave them.

No Big Deal!

The disciples couldn't believe that it was Jesus who was walking on top of the very thing that was about to destroy them:

> *But when they saw him walking upon the sea, they supposed it had been a spirit, and cried out.*
>
> Mark 6:49

The disciples concluded, *This can't be Jesus. He can't walk on the water!* When we're overwhelmed by a storm, it can cause us to miss the Lord and not draw on His supernatural ability. It's because we can't imagine that He is greater than what is coming against us.

Another time the disciples did not recognize Jesus is recorded in Luke 24. Some of them were walking on the road to Emmaus with the risen Lord; but just like in Mark 6, they didn't know it was Him. They couldn't imagine that He had risen from the dead. The Bible says they were preoccupied with being sad over Jesus' suffering and crucifixion (Luke 24:17–24). When Jesus asked what they were sad about, they seemed to criticize Him, almost as if He ought to know how terrible things were and that He should be as upset as they were.

Many times, when we're going through something, we think the Lord should be up in heaven wringing His hands, saying, "This is a really big problem!" Some people say, "Oh, man, we need to fast and pray! We need lots of people. It's going to take two, three, or four hundred people on the prayer chain praying because this is such a big deal! If God provides this miracle, all the lights of heaven are going to dim!" But that's never the case. Sometimes we live so much in the natural realm that we ask, "God, is there really a way out of this?" We need to understand that there's always a way out. Whatever our situation is, Jesus is on top of it. Nothing is too difficult for Him. Really, it's no big deal!

Be of Good Cheer

The disciples were not novices about boating. At least four of them—Peter, Andrew, James, and John—were fishermen. These were not men who were easily frightened on the water. They knew that they were in a serious situation. Yet, in the midst of this crisis situation, Jesus told the disciples, *"Be of good cheer: it is I; be not afraid"* (Mark 6:50b).

You might be in the same position the disciples were in when the Lord told them to be of good cheer. If the Lord had instead magnified the problem, spoken in unbelief, or talked about how bad things were for them, they would have stayed in trouble. Jesus needed to minimize the situation, magnify God, and show them that His power was so much greater than their circumstances. He did that by walking on top of the very thing that could have destroyed them.

Now, most people won't be of good cheer until they see their physical problems resolved. Then, when everything works out, they'll be of good cheer. But faith doesn't work that way. You must first get into faith, resist fear, and be of good cheer while the storm is still raging, and the ship is going down. Then you will see the miracle.

Think of it this way: If all the Lord wanted was for His disciples to be of good cheer, then He could have stilled the storm first, and then their joy would have come. But He told them to be of good cheer before He stilled the storm. He was basically telling them, "Trust Me. Don't you remember who I am? I'm the one who just miraculously fed the multitude with just a tiny bit of food. I'm the one who has already seen the dead raised, blind eyes and deaf ears opened, and demons cast out!" If the disciples had recognized who was with them, they would have had faith. God is trying to get a response of faith from us today. Anyone can be of good cheer and overcome fear after the storm stops and everything works out. But a greater blessing is on us if we believe before we see.

> *Jesus saith unto him, Thomas, because thou hast seen me, thou hast believed: blessed are they that have not seen, and yet have believed.*
>
> John 20:29

If you're in the midst of a storm in your life, if your boat is filling up with water, if you feel like you're about to drown, Jesus would tell you to not be afraid but to be of good cheer. If you really understand this truth, it's enough to make you shout! It'll cause you to stand up on the inside; and once you do, then eventually you'll stand up on the outside too. That's when you'll see your physical circumstances change. That's when you'll walk on the water!

Chapter 3

Flying in the Face of the Storm

These disciples had a command from the Lord Jesus Christ. They didn't go across the sea on their own. It was Jesus' will; it wasn't theirs:

> *And straightway Jesus constrained his disciples to get into a ship, and to go before him unto the other side.*
>
> Matthew 14:22

Constrained means that Jesus had to use some force. He didn't physically grab his disciples and throw them into the boat. However, they did express some type of resistance toward getting in and setting sail. So, Jesus constrained them, which basically means He forcefully told them, "Get in and go!"

Why did the disciples resist? Why did Jesus have to constrain them? Many of these men had grown up as fishermen on the Sea of Galilee. This body of water is famous for having storms come down over the mountains that are to the east of it.1 These mountains tend to hide storms until they crest over the tops. Then the storms can quickly rush down upon the sea. So, you'd really have to be in tune with what the weather was like.

The Weather Report

Most of us only know what the weather is like by listening to a weatherman. We have virtually no awareness whatsoever. I remember pastoring a little group of ranchers in Pritchett, Colorado, and they would say, "Well, it's going to rain tonight."

I'd ask, "Did you hear that on the weather report?"

They'd say, "No." They just felt the barometric pressure changing and the humidity in the air. Sure enough, it would be exactly as they'd said. They would tell me, "That wind is coming out of the north. That means we're going to have a northerner come in." These guys were much better than the weatherman at predicting the weather. After being around these guys for just a short period of time, I began picking up on these things too. Soon I was able to tell when a winter storm was coming in.

These disciples were far more in tune with the weather than we are today. That's why Jesus had to constrain them. That storm may not have hit yet, but all the signs were there. It was against their better judgment to be out on the Sea of Galilee at that time. Yet they went because Jesus told them to.

Against their better judgment, they went out on the sea at the command of the Lord. They were in this situation because of obedience to the Lord. That's important.

Adversity in God's Will

In Matthew 14, Jesus' disciples had a word from God, but that didn't mean they wouldn't have any problems. Remember, the winds were contrary, and the disciples were struggling to get to the other side. Nevertheless, they were perfectly in the center of God's will. They voiced their doubts, but the Lord—knowing full well what their doubts were—said, "No, you go to the other side. It'll work!" God's Word will fly in the face of life's storms.

So, you can be perfectly led by God and still experience hardship. Satan will come against you. There will be circumstances in your life that will look like you're not going to make it, but that's not always a sign that you've missed God.

It's also important for you to realize that the adversity you're suffering may be the result of your own ignorance or disobedience. For instance, Jonah ran away from God. Instead of following the Lord's instructions, he rebelled and got caught in a storm that almost cost him his life!

You need to be honest enough to evaluate where you are. Is your situation the result of your own rebellion toward God? Did you or did you not have a word from Him when you left the shore?

Call Out to God

If you have a word from God, stand on it full of good cheer because He is with you. Don't be afraid. Exercise your faith before you see the outcome. Faith is seeing the miracle manifest in your heart before you see it manifest in the physical realm. Start praising, worshiping, and rejoicing before you win your battle.

Call out to God! Don't just sit there in silence and let your problems overtake you. But don't call out in unbelief like the disciples did when Jesus walked on the water, and they thought He was a ghost. Don't cry out in frustration, anger, or bitterness. Call out to Him in faith! Make a demand. Draw on the power of God that is available to you. Have faith and be of good courage. Then let your faith abound in thanksgiving (Col. 2:6–7). You're laying the groundwork for the miracle God is about to perform on your behalf.

Something else that is very important in this story is that they were still headed in the direction the Lord told them to go. Although the wind was against them and it looked like they might drown, they hadn't turned around and headed back to where they came from. With such a strong wind buffeting them, they could have turned around, hoisted the sail, and made it back to safety in no time.

In order to receive a miracle like they did, you have to be positioned to receive that miracle. Those who cling to the safety of the shore will never be water walkers.

Chapter 4

Peter's Positive Response

And Peter answered him and said, Lord, if it be thou, bid me come unto thee on the water.

Matthew 14:28

Remember, at this point the disciples had spent somewhere between seven and twelve hours trying to get across the Sea of Galilee. Normally, this entire trip would have taken about two or three hours; but they were only halfway across the lake. In the midst of all this, Jesus came walking on the water. They saw Him and cried out in fear. Jesus basically said, "Guys, be of good cheer. It's Me. Don't be afraid!" Peter then responded, *"If it be thou, bid me come unto thee on the water."* This encounter with the Lord affected Peter in a supernatural way. Peter was able to disregard the storm and the boat and focus on the miraculous power and ability of God.

In order to become a water walker, you must first get out of the boat. The boat is whatever you trust in to take you to the other side. The boat is what everyone else has come to depend on. Many would like the supernatural experience of walking on water, but they don't want to depart from the relative safety of their boat.

Ironically, the boat the disciples were in was full of water and sinking. Yet, Peter was the only one willing to step out of the boat and try walking on water. It's amazing that the other disciples were so afraid to get out of the boat. It was full of water and going down, yet they were clinging to something that couldn't save them. Likewise, it amazes me how we put so much trust in natural things when they aren't working.

The world is locked into ways of coping with life's problems that don't work. Like the lepers of 2 Kings 7, what have you got to lose? How long are you going to sit there, until you die? To be a water walker, you've got to take a risk. You've got to get out of the boat that the rest of the world is drowning in and step out on faith.

Destroyed or Motivated?

Peter was in the same situation the other disciples were in; however, when Jesus appeared, he started believing God. He began thinking, *If Jesus can walk on water, then I can too*. He responded positively. If you're going to be a water walker, you must get your focus off your circumstances and look to God for something more! That's what Peter did. He was able to look past the storm—those things in the natural—and focus his attention on Jesus.

Are you able to look past the circumstances in your life? Can you get out of your boat of self-pity and look to the Lord? Are you able to look past your situation and see that God is victorious and well able to help you overcome? Or are you going to sit there and let the circumstances of life overcome you?

You must answer these questions if you are going to see miracles in your life. You must first lift your head up and start looking for something else. You have to hope that there is something more than what you're experiencing. Shake yourself out of the frustration, discouragement, and despair! Decide that you're going to overcome. God's power is truly what delivers you, but that power is activated by what you choose to believe. Peter called out to Jesus and started making a demand on the Lord's power. Will you do the same?

How Are You Asking?

Although Peter had good intentions, notice that in Matthew 14:28, he basically asked Jesus, "If it's you, bid me come to You on the water." Peter desired to do what Jesus was doing and walk in the miraculous. However, the way he asked was incorrect.

How else could Jesus have answered him? "Wait, Peter, it's not Me—don't come"? What if it really wasn't God's plan for Peter to walk on water? It's certainly possible it wasn't God's best. However, the way Peter asked this question didn't leave Jesus with many ways to answer it.

If Peter had asked this question differently and said, "Lord, do You want me to walk on the water with You?" it's possible he could have received a different answer. Jesus could have responded, "Well, Peter, I'll come to you. Then we'll go to the other side, and everything will be just fine."

"Come!"

While we don't know what could've happened, we do know that Jesus simply told Peter, *"Come"* (Matt. 14:29a). If you are believing God for something miraculous and are about to take the biggest step of your life, make sure that it's God leading you to do it instead of you backing God into a corner and leaving Him no other option.

Are you asking God something like, "Do You want me to serve You by being in full-time ministry or not to serve You at all?" Well, if that's the way you phrase your question, God's going to say, "Serve Me." But it's possible that He would prefer you to stay in the business world and serve Him that way. You need to be careful that what you're stepping out of the boat and believing for is truly God leading you and not just a result of misunderstanding or confusion.

When you're sure of what God is saying to you, there is more than enough power in His Word to overcome any problem you may have—sickness, finances, relationship, etc. But you must step out and act on it in faith. There was enough power in God's Word for every one of the disciples to walk on the water. Yet they probably didn't get out of the boat because of fear. They simply refused to take that step of faith. Make the decision today that whatever God speaks to you, you're going to believe.

Chapter 5

Get Out of the Boat

Peter got out of the boat and *"walked on the water, to go to Jesus"* (Matt. 14:29b). He'd taken his attention off the winds and waves— everything that was hindering him from making it to the other side—and was looking at Jesus.

One word from Jesus—*"Come"*— was enough to overcome the storm that was trying to destroy Peter! The good news is that there are lots of words in the Bible. Just one word quickened— made alive—to us is enough to overcome any storm or problem we may encounter in life. It's not the quantity of words that makes the difference but rather how much we value God's Word. That's powerful!

I've sat next to people in services who listened to the exact same message I did, and they may have been a little blessed, but then they just went about their lives without realizing how powerful the word they heard really was. Yet I sat there and was impacted to the point that I took that word and meditated on it until it exploded on the inside of me. We all have the same ability to receive God's Word, but the value we place on it determines its impact.

What Is Your Boat?

When you are called to step out of your boat—whatever it is—you can see what you're leaving, but not what you would miss if you decided to stay in the boat instead. In other words, hindsight gives you the ability to look back and see what it cost you to serve God, but you don't have the ability to look forward and see what you'll be missing if you don't serve Him. God is a good God. He'll never require more of you than what He gives to you. You'll always be more blessed in following the Lord than you ever would be in not following Him. But you must be willing to identify what is holding you back—your boat—and step out of it!

Many people are so afraid of failure that they continue to stay in the situation they're in, which guarantees their failure. If you aren't stretching yourself and believing God for something bigger than what you can produce on your own, you're already a failure. I don't say this to condemn or hurt you, but rather to challenge you. God is a supernatural God! God is a big God!

[God is] *able to do exceeding abundantly above all that we ask or think, according to the power that worketh in us.*
Ephesians 3:20

Is your life "normal" according to the world's system? Can anyone tell the difference between you and your neighbor? Do you go to the doctor as often as they do? Do you have the same number of bills and debt as they do? Do you have the same worries and cares as they do? Does it bother you the same as it does your unsaved friend when negative things happen in this world? If so, you need to recognize something is seriously wrong. There should be something different about you compared to your unsaved neighbor.

Before you can see the miraculous power of God manifest in your life, you need to make a conscious decision to leave the safety of the boat. You must get out of your comfort zone. The fear of being different and the desire to be safe are real faith killers.

Yea, they turned back and tempted God, and limited the Holy One of Israel.

Psalm 78:41

You limit God by not having a vision, by not taking a step of faith, or by being unwilling to take a risk. Fear limits God—fearing the unknown, fearing failure, or fearing change. Thinking small or being lazy will limit what God can do in your life. You need to take the limits off of Him if you're going to walk in the miraculous!

Try Something New

If you're the type of person who wants your whole life planned out and simply refuses to take a risk, then you'll never walk on water. If you insist on knowing exactly where you'll be, what you'll be doing, and who you will be doing it with twenty years from now, you'll never see God's best. It takes faith to see the real super-natural power of God.

A good friend of mine says, "God will usually terrify you before He edifies you!" God's vision for your life will be bigger than what you can do on your own, and it will overwhelm you. My friend also says, "If your dreams and visions don't keep you up at night, you're thinking too small!" If it's God, He'll call you to do something that's beyond your ability. He'll call you to be a water walker—to walk on top of the impossible situation that's facing you. You'll have to get out of the boat in order to respond to God in faith!

Part of being a water walker is being willing to get out of the safety of the boat. You have to depart from what's familiar and what everybody else is doing. You must be willing to try something new. Step out and take a chance!

Chapter 6

Out on the Limb

Some people just can't transition from trusting the so-called security the world has to offer to risking the unknown by getting out of the boat. However, fruit grows out on the limb! Most of us want to hold onto the trunk and still have all the fruit that comes from being out on the limb, but it doesn't work that way. You need to get out there where you're bobbing up and down in the breeze. You need to feel that insecurity of wobbling around and wondering, *Is this thing going to hold me or not?* That's where the fruit grows.

Some people never get out into the deep; they refuse to lose sight of the shore. They won't get in above their ankles because they're afraid of what might be out there. If you knew the water was only six inches deep, you wouldn't mind getting out of the boat because you'd know there's no real danger. However, one of the aspects of truly getting out of the boat is not knowing how deep the water is and dealing with the fear of the unknown and being willing to trust the results—the future and the unknown—to God.

When you get out of the boat and start believing God for something big, you will start seeing miracles. I've spent more than five decades stepping out of the boat, and I still get excited every time I do something big! I've continually taken new steps of faith that make previous ones look small. If the Lord doesn't come through, we're sunk. But I have faith that the best is yet to come. I'll never go back to playing it safe. I'm going for it!

You might say, "Andrew, you shouldn't say that. What happens if it doesn't come to pass?" Well, what happens if it *does* come to pass? I've seen God come through so many times that I'm not worried. I know He's not limited. The only limitation He has is me.

Afraid of Failure

"So, what if, like Peter, I don't do it perfectly? What happens if I only walk part of the way? What would happen if only part of my vision comes to pass? What happens if I shoot for the stars but only hit the moon?" Some people would look at that as failure, but I'd say you did pretty good.

Many people are afraid of failure and what other people might say. Yet I think the people who are the biggest failures are those who do nothing. If you shoot at nothing and hit it every time, that's a failure!

Faith Pleases God

Although Peter walked on the water, people today criticize him because he began to sink. However, other than Jesus, Peter's the only person who has ever physically walked on water! He may not have done it perfectly, but he did it. I believe God was thrilled when he stepped out and walked on the water.

But without faith it is impossible to please him: for he that cometh to God must believe that he is, and that he is a rewarder of them that diligently seek him.

Hebrews 11:6

When Peter began to sink, instead of God saying, "You didn't do it perfectly. You failed," I believe the Lord exclaimed, "Peter actually walked on water!" I believe God was thrilled to see one of His children out there trying! He was pleased that Peter stepped out in faith.

Get Up and Try Again

We may fail. When we get out of the boat, we run the risk of sinking. Peter didn't go all the way under the water, but he began to sink (Matt. 14:30), and Jesus had to rescue him. The good news is that He delivered Peter. He didn't push him under, saying, "You sorry thing. I'll teach you for not believing hard enough!" Instead, the Lord reached out and lifted him up.

If you fail, Jesus will be there. Even though people may be hard on you and say, "Well, you could've done better," Jesus will encourage you to keep trying. He'll say, "I'm so proud of you. Go for it! Get up and try again!"

It's similar to when we teach our children to ride a bike. When they try and fail, we don't tell them they are stupid and didn't do it right. No! We tell them, "You went ten feet. You did good. Try it again."

If you're making changes out of your own presumption because you aren't waiting on God, His way, and His timing, then that's a different situation. But if you're acting out of a pure heart and can truthfully say, "Father, I'm doing this because I believe with all my heart that this is You leading me to take a step of faith and move in this direction," then go for it! Even if you think you will fail, you won't. You'll be a success in God's eyes!

Follow His Leading

When we stand before God and He judges us for what happened in our lifetimes, I believe we'll be surprised. God's going to look at some people whom the world considered failures and say, "You stepped out in faith and were trying to obey Me." Faith is what pleases God!

If you could somehow "succeed" without trusting God, you've failed. You may have money, prestige, honor, recognition, possessions, and influence; but if you haven't really trusted God and stepped out to do what He wanted you to do, then you've failed. You might be considered a great success in the eyes of man, but God will look at you and say, "You failed to do what I told you to do."

On the other hand, there will be people who didn't amount to much in the eyes of the world. They didn't have much, yet they trusted God. They believed Him and did what He told them to do. The Lord will say to them, *"Well done, good and faithful servant . . ."* (Matt. 25:23). God never bases His evaluation of faithfulness only on the outcome but by whether or not you were following His leading. That's encouraging!

If the Lord tarries, someday in the future people may talk about how you trusted God when you stepped out in obedience to Him. You can be an inspiration to somebody else the way Peter is to so many Christians. If Peter had stayed in the boat, no one would be discussing him walking on the water. This story wouldn't have been in the Bible. Praise God he had enough faith to trust God. I admire Peter for being able to look beyond himself, trust Jesus, and step out on the water. It's awesome! And I believe it was written as an example of what you can do too!

Chapter 7

Little Faith

Everybody wants to walk on water, but nobody wants to get out of the boat. They're worried about what could happen or what others will think. The truth is, there *will* be challenges if you do what God tells you to do. However, there will also be challenges if you *don't* do what He tells you to do. Why not just do what He says? If you accept the line of thinking that ultimately keeps you in the boat, you'll never see the miraculous like Peter did. I believe "stinkin' thinkin'" is one of the biggest obstacles you'll face as a believer, and it's one of the quickest ways to short-circuit the power of God in your life. It'll stop you every time if you let it.

Now let's look at the opposition Peter faced when he stepped out of the boat:

> *But when he saw the wind boisterous, he was afraid; and beginning to sink, he cried, saying, Lord, save me.*
>
> Matthew 14:30

On the surface, it might be easy to relate to Peter's fear here, but what did the boisterous wind have to do with him walking on the water? Nothing. If Peter had kept his eyes on Jesus, the Author and Finisher of his faith (Heb. 12:2), he would have walked on water all the way to the Lord. Then he could have walked with Jesus back to the boat, or the shore, or anywhere else he wanted to go. He had already proven that he could walk on the water. He had already defied the laws of nature and was walking by faith. In the natural, he couldn't have walked on the water if it had been a perfectly calm day. The wind was just something that took his attention away from Jesus.

When Peter took his eyes off the Lord and began to look at the wind and the waves, he started focusing on the natural realm. His mind was probably flooded with thoughts like, *You shouldn't be out here. This is crazy. You can't do this.* Like most people, he was comfortable in the safety of the boat, and he trusted it. This is easy to understand, but it's what caused Peter to sink.

Little Unbelief Is the Key

When he began to sink, Peter cried out,

Lord, save me. And immediately Jesus stretched forth his hand, and caught him, and said unto him, O thou of little faith, wherefore didst thou doubt?

Matthew 14:30b–31

Notice how Jesus said that Peter had *"little faith."* Most people believe that to do something miraculous, you must have big faith, great faith, or tons of faith. But the Lord said Peter had little faith. Yet, as long as "little faith" was focused on Jesus, it was enough to walk on water!

Jesus brought up an important truth here that most Christians haven't really understood because they're too busy trying to build their faith to get "big" faith. However, the key to the Christian life isn't "big" faith but rather "little" unbelief.

Dealing with Unbelief

Very few Christians understand how important dealing with unbelief is when walking in miracles. I believe that if Peter had dealt with his unbelief properly, he never would have started to sink. You see, most Christians believe that if you just increase your faith, then unbelief will disappear. The disciples felt the same way:

And the apostles said unto the Lord, Increase our faith. And the Lord said, If ye had faith as a grain of mustard seed, ye might say unto this sycamine tree, Be thou plucked up by the root, and be thou planted in the sea; and it should obey you.

Luke 17:5–6

In other words, Jesus was saying, "Guys, you don't need more faith. Your faith is sufficient. If your faith is only the size of a mustard seed, it's enough to uproot a tree without touching it. Just by speaking to it, you could make this tree move."

If you could understand this, it would answer some of the questions you've probably had, like, "I know I believed, so why didn't it work?" It's not because you weren't believing; it's because you were believing and disbelieving at the same time! Miracles don't require huge amounts of faith—just a pure and simple faith that isn't negated by unbelief.

Monitor Your Ometers

Imagine two meters. One is a faith-ometer, and the other is an unbelief-ometer. We need to constantly monitor both of them. Most people don't even acknowledge the amount of unbelief in their lives; they just think that having fear, worry, or stress is normal. Then they try to build faith by reading the Word, praying, and fasting.

There isn't anything wrong with these things, but they don't increase your faith. You've already got all the faith that you need:

For I say, through the grace given unto me, to every man that is among you, not to think of himself more highly than he ought to think; but to think soberly, according as God hath dealt to every man the measure of faith.

Romans 12:3

God provided faith two thousand years ago through the atonement of the Lord Jesus Christ. Your prayer and fasting won't move Him to give you more; they'll only move you.

However, once you remove unbelief, faith won't be a problem. It'll flow freely. Miracles will start happening. It'll begin to work.

Chapter 8

Dealing with Unbelief

It's important to understand that there are three kinds of unbelief:

1. **Ignorance:** Unbelief can come from a lack of knowledge. For instance, some people have never heard about miracles because they've never read the Bible. They've been taught from the time they were kids that the physical realm is all there is—that there isn't a spiritual world or anything beyond the natural realm. You could tell them about the Word of God, yet they would resist it because they've never heard of this before. The antidote to this kind of unbelief, caused by ignorance, is simply to tell them the truth. If they embrace it, the truth will set them free.

   And ye shall know the truth, and the truth shall make you free.

   John 8:32

2. **Wrong teaching:** The second type of unbelief is one that comes through wrong teaching. It's not a *lack* of knowledge, but it's *wrong* knowledge. Growing up, I was taught that miracles passed away with the apostles and that God doesn't do them today. That's the kind of wrong teaching that made me resistant to miracles and believing God for them.

The antidote for this is the same—the truth. Now, ignorance is easier to overcome than wrong teaching. You must reject the wrong teaching and then start the process of embracing the right teaching. It's more difficult, but it's basically the same process. You tell someone the truth, and it will set them free if they believe it.

3. **Natural unbelief:** But the third kind of unbelief—natural unbelief—comes through your five senses. It was this type of natural unbelief that Jesus was talking about in the case of a demonized boy in Matthew 17.

Then Jesus answered and said, O faithless and perverse generation, how long shall I be with you? how long shall I suffer you? bring him hither to me. And Jesus rebuked the devil; and he departed out of him: and the child was cured from that very hour. Then came the disciples to Jesus apart, and said, Why could not we cast him out? And Jesus said unto them, Because of your unbelief: for verily I say unto you, If ye have faith as a grain of mustard seed, ye shall say unto this mountain, Remove hence to yonder place; and it shall remove; and nothing shall be impossible unto you. Howbeit this kind goeth not out but by prayer and fasting.

Matthew 17:17–21

When they brought this boy to Jesus, the child fell to the ground, wallowed, and foamed at the mouth (Mark 9:20). Apparently, these disciples had seen demons cast out before, but they hadn't seen a manifestation quite like this. Their senses—what they saw and heard—triggered thoughts, feelings, and emotions opposite of their faith in the power and authority Jesus gave them.

And when he had called unto him *his twelve disciples, he gave them power* against *unclean spirits, to cast them out, and to heal all manner of sickness and all manner of disease.*

Matthew 10:1

Then he called his twelve disciples together, and gave them power and authority over all devils, and to cure diseases.

Luke 9:1

The disciples spoke, but what they saw and heard made it look like this demon wasn't going to respond. So, they had unbelief come through their senses. They had faith, which is why they spoke and were puzzled about not seeing the healing come to pass; but they were still too sensitive to their physical senses.

Dealing with Unbelief 43

Train Your Senses

Your five senses aren't evil. God gave them to you for good and you need your five physical senses to function in this world. For example, it'd be hard to get around if you couldn't see. If you were to drive me somewhere in your car, I'd want you to act on what you see with your eyes. I wouldn't want you to drive by faith!

However, at times, God will call you to do things that go against your five senses. When He does, how will you respond? The answer to that question depends largely upon your relationship with Him. Have you been spending time with Him, specifically in prayer and fasting? This is how you begin to train your five senses.

But strong meat belongeth to them . . . who by reason of use have their senses exercised to discern both good and evil.

Hebrews 5:14

Your five senses can be exercised (trained) to discern things beyond just their physical, natural ability. If you spend time with the Lord in fasting and prayer, you can train your mind to respond in faith. If you spend a lot of time with the Lord, you'll start hearing from Him, you'll start seeing miracles, and you'll have evidence of the reality of the spiritual world. There will be physical proof that the Word of God works.

Over a period of time, even if you can't physically perceive something that is consistent with what you're believing for, your mind can be trained to say, "Well, I can't see, taste, hear, smell, or feel it, but I've spent so much time with the Lord and have seen Him come through on so many occasions, I know there is more." This is how it works for me. I'm not perfect at it, and it hasn't come about easily, but I am no longer limited by my five senses. I believe God. You can, too!

Exercise Yourself

Notice that Hebrews 5:14 says that their senses were exercised *"by reason of use."* This word *"exercised"* is very important. You don't just get up and start preparing for a marathon the morning of the race. You must exercise regularly!

Many Christians don't really spend much time with the Lord. Instead, they focus on the physical realm, working a job and watching television. They do everything in the natural realm, spending virtually no time praying and fellowshipping with God or fasting and denying their senses. Then they get into a crisis situation and chase after a miracle with all they have. They're 100 percent sincere and genuinely dedicated, but it's too little too late. They haven't exercised (trained) themselves. Some people even die, not because they were believing wrong, but because they run out of time before their faith can catch up to and overtake their senses.

This is why fasting works. Fasting is simply denying the five senses because hunger is affected by them all. It's very powerful. If you're someone who is dominated and controlled by your five senses, and if they are more real to you than what God says, then fasting is how you can change that.

Who's Controlling Who?

Within just a few hours of when you start fasting, you'll get hungry, and your body will begin complaining and trying to regain control. Your appetite will try to dominate and force you to eat. If you stick with it and say, "Nope, I'm going to believe God. Man does not live by bread alone, but by every word that proceeds from the mouth of God" (Matt. 4:4), your body will rebel. It will try to control you.

If you just continue, saying, "Well, then, I'm going to fast all day," your body will respond, "All day? I'll be dead by evening!"

You answer, "All right, we'll go two days," to which your body will reply, "No, I'll never last two days!"

"All right, three days!"

Pretty soon, your body will learn that it will have to submit. When you fast over a prolonged period of time, after about two or three days of denying your appetite, you'll actually reach a point where you aren't hungry anymore. Your senses won't bother you. You can get to a place where you aren't missing food anymore because your appetite is under control.

Then, if sickness attacks your body, you can say, "I'm healed in the name of Jesus." If your body doesn't instantaneously manifest that healing and you're still in pain, you can tell your body, "I'm not going by what I feel." If you've been fasting and praying—denying yourself and spending time in the presence of God—you've trained yourself to say, "What I believe is just as real as what I see, taste, hear, smell, and feel." Your body will respond to that. You'll be able to stay the course and stand in faith until you see the manifestation of your healing.

But if you haven't been spending time in the spiritual realm, if you've just been totally dominated by the physical realm and you say, "Body, you're healed. I don't care what you feel," your senses will answer, "Who are you to tell me anything? I tell you when to eat, what to eat, and how much to eat." Since you haven't trained your senses, they'll control you instead of you controlling them. When you pray, your five senses are going to ask, "Who are you talking to? I can't see anybody. I can't hear anyone. I don't feel anybody here." But if you persist in prayer and relationship with God, your senses will line up, and your heart will become sensitive to God. It's just that simple!

Conclusion

Peter was able to walk on the water because he got out of the boat and simply started walking to Jesus. While Peter kept his eyes on the Lord, he was able to do the supernatural and walk on top of something that would have killed other people. But when Peter looked at the wind around him and took his eyes off Jesus, unbelief came. The wind wasn't sin. It wasn't terrible. It was just natural, and it made Peter relate back to the natural. He still had faith, but unbelief crept in when he considered natural things.

Recognize that you are supernatural, and that God wants to meet your needs in a supernatural way. When you keep your eyes on Jesus, you can walk in health, prosperity, joy, and peace. You can do the supernatural things that God calls you to do. You don't need to be limited by natural solutions to your problems.

All of us have natural things that are going to tell us that the Word of God doesn't work. If you can't see, taste, hear, smell, or feel it, your senses will try to convince you it doesn't exist. You are going to have to train yourself (exercise your senses) to know there's more to life than the physical realm.

Remember, you can get rid of two types of unbelief—ignorance and wrong teaching—just by hearing the truth and believing it. But the only way you can overcome your five senses and the unbelief they cause is through fasting and prayer (Matt. 17:21).

You can become a water walker. If you are facing a problem you are struggling to overcome, it's because you have more unbelief than faith. It doesn't take great faith. It takes a simple faith, a pure faith, a faith that isn't counterbalanced by unbelief. Once you deal with that unbelief, you *will* walk on water!

FURTHER STUDY

If you enjoyed this booklet and would like to learn more about some of the things I've shared, I suggest my teachings:

- *Hardness of Heart*
- *Spiritual Authority*
- *How to Receive a Miracle*
- *You've Already Got It!*
- *Don't Limit God*

These teachings are available for free at **awmi.net**, or they can be purchased at **awmi.net/store**.

Go deeper in your relationship with God by browsing all of Andrew's free teachings.

Receive Jesus as Your Savior

Choosing to receive Jesus Christ as your Lord and Savior is the most important decision you'll ever make!

God's Word promises, *"That if thou shalt confess with thy mouth the Lord Jesus, and shalt believe in thine heart that God hath raised him from the dead, thou shalt be saved. For with the heart man believeth unto righteousness; and with the mouth confession is made unto salvation"* (Rom. 10:9–10). *"For whosoever shall call upon the name of the Lord shall be saved"* (Rom. 10:13). By His grace, God has already done everything to provide salvation. Your part is simply to believe and receive.

Pray out loud: "Jesus, I acknowledge that I've sinned and need to receive what you did for the forgiveness of my sins. I confess that You are my Lord and Savior. I believe in my heart that God raised You from the dead. By faith in Your Word, I receive salvation now. Thank You for saving me."

The very moment you commit your life to Jesus Christ, the truth of His Word instantly comes to pass in your spirit. Now that you're born again, there's a brand-new you!

Please contact us and let us know that you've prayed to receive Jesus as your Savior. We'd like to send you some free materials to help you on your new journey. Call our Helpline: **719-635-1111** (available 24 hours a day, seven days a week) to speak to a staff member who is here to help you understand and grow in your new relationship with the Lord.

Welcome to your new life!

Receive the Holy Spirit

As His child, your loving heavenly Father wants to give you the supernatural power you need to live a new life. *"For every one that asketh receiveth; and he that seeketh findeth; and to him that knocketh it shall be opened…how much more shall* your *heavenly Father give the Holy Spirit to them that ask him?"* (Luke 11:10–13).

All you have to do is ask, believe, and receive!

Pray this: "Father, I recognize my need for Your power to live a new life. Please fill me with Your Holy Spirit. By faith, I receive it right now. Thank You for baptizing me. Holy Spirit, You are welcome in my life."

Some syllables from a language you don't recognize will rise up from your heart to your mouth (1 Cor. 14:14). As you speak them out loud by faith, you're releasing God's power from within and building yourself up in the spirit (1 Cor. 14:4). You can do this whenever and wherever you like.

It doesn't really matter whether you felt anything or not when you prayed to receive the Lord and His Spirit. If you believed in your heart that you received, then God's Word promises you did. *"Therefore I say unto you, What things soever ye desire, when ye pray, believe that ye receive* them*, and ye shall have* them" (Mark 11:24). God always honors His Word—believe it!

We would like to rejoice with you, pray with you, and answer any questions to help you understand more fully what has taken place in your life!

Please contact us to let us know that you've prayed to be filled with the Holy Spirit and to request the book *The New You & the Holy Spirit*. This book will explain in more detail about the benefits of being filled with the Holy Spirit and speaking in tongues. Call our Helpline: **719-635-1111** (available 24 hours a day, seven days a week).

Call for Prayer

If you need prayer for any reason, you can call our Helpline, 24 hours a day, seven days a week at **719-635-1111**. A trained prayer minister will answer your call and pray with you.

Every day, we receive testimonies of healings and other miracles from our Helpline, and we are ministering God's nearly-too-good-to-be-true message of the Gospel to more people than ever. So, I encourage you to call today!

About the Author

Andrew Wommack's life was forever changed the moment he encountered the supernatural love of God on March 23, 1968. As a renowned Bible teacher and author, Andrew has made it his mission to change the way the world sees God.

Andrew's vision is to go as far and deep with the Gospel as possible. His message goes far through the *Gospel Truth* television program, which is available to over half the world's population. The message goes deep through discipleship at Charis Bible College, headquartered in Woodland Park, Colorado. Founded in 1994, Charis has campuses across the United States and around the globe.

Andrew also has an extensive library of teaching materials in print, audio, and video. More than 200,000 hours of free teachings can be accessed at **awmi.net**.

Endnotes

1. "Sea of Galilee." BibleGateway. Accessed October 3, 2023.
    https://www.biblegateway.com/resources/encyclopedia-of-
    the-bible/Sea-Galilee.

Contact Information

Andrew Wommack Ministries, Inc.
PO Box 3333
Colorado Springs, CO 80934-3333
info@awmi.net
awmi.net

Helpline: 719-635-1111 (available 24/7)

Charis Bible College
info@charisbiblecollege.org
844-360-9577
CharisBibleCollege.org

For a complete list of all of our offices,
visit **awmi.net/contact-us**.

Connect with us on social media.